T0379238

I Got a Pet!

My Pet Ferret

By Brienna Rossiter

level 2
little blue readers

www.littlebluehousebooks.com

Copyright © 2023 by Little Blue House, Mendota Heights, MN 55120. All rights reserved. No part of this book may be reproduced or utilized in any form or by any means without written permission from the publisher.

Little Blue House is distributed by North Star Editions:
sales@northstareditions.com | 888-417-0195

Produced for Little Blue House by Red Line Editorial.

Photographs ©: Shutterstock Images, cover, 6–7, 8, 11, 18–19, 21, 23, 24 (top right), 24 (bottom right); iStockphoto, 4, 13, 14–15, 16, 24 (top left), 24 (bottom left)

Library of Congress Control Number: 2022901881

ISBN
978-1-64619-587-9 (hardcover)
978-1-64619-614-2 (paperback)
978-1-64619-666-1 (ebook pdf)
978-1-64619-641-8 (hosted ebook)

Printed in the United States of America
Mankato, MN
082022

About the Author

Brienna Rossiter is a writer and editor who lives in Minnesota.

Table of Contents

My Pet Ferret **5**

Playtime **9**

Ferret Care **17**

Glossary **24**

Index **24**

My Pet Ferret

I have a ferret.

It is a good pet.

My ferret lives in a
big cage.
The cage has two levels.
My ferret climbs up
and down.

Playtime

I put toys inside the cage.

My ferret plays with the toys.

I take my ferret out of the cage to play with it.
I hold my ferret.

My ferret is active.

It likes to run and bounce.

I give my ferret exercise.

I let it run around

my house.

Sometimes I take my ferret outside. It wears a harness and a leash.

Ferret Care

My ferret eats meat.

It eats pellets, too.

I put my ferret's food

in a bowl.

My ferret drinks water.
I change the water to
keep it fresh.
I make sure it does not
run out.

My ferret needs attention.
I play with it every day.
That way, it will not get
bored or lonely.

My ferret also
needs sleep.
It has a soft bed inside
its cage.

Glossary

ferret

leash

harness

pellets

Index

B
bed, 22

C
cage, 6, 9–10, 22

F
food, 17

T
toys, 9

24